The Beginners' Guide to Writing, Self-Publishing and Marketing a Book

The Beginners' Guide to Writing, Self-Publishing and Marketing a Book

Kehinde Adesina & Taiwo Adesina

Copyright Notice

Copyright © 2012 Kehinde Adesina, Taiwo Adesina

Published—2013

ISBN: 978-1-909787-14-8

Published by Purpose2Destiny TK Limited

All rights reserved. Any unauthorized broadcasting, public performance, copying or recording will constitute an infringement of copyright. Permission granted to reproduce for personal and educational use only. Commercial copying, hiring, lending is prohibited.

Some Authors have been quoted or referred to in this book, their rights are preserved and the writers of this book do not seek to infringe on those rights.

This work is registered with the UK Copyright Service

Exclusion of Liability and Disclaimer

The authors shall have neither liability nor responsibility to any person or entity with respect to any loss or damage caused or alleged to be caused directly or indirectly by the information covered in this Book. This book is meant to guide you through the process of writing, publishing and marketing your book.

Although careful precaution has been taken in the preparation of this material, the authors assume no liability for any incidental, consequential or other liability from the use of this information. All risks and damages, incidental or otherwise, arising from the use or misuse of the information contained herein are entirely the responsibility of the reader.

Acknowledgement

We thank Traci Shoblom for her initial input and editing of this Manuscript. We also thank Malcolm Havard, a published author of non-fiction and a novelist, for his input into this book.

Photography by Gemsjummy, Jumoke Ademola has been a professional photographer for many years.

Contents

PREFACE xi

PART 1 – A GUIDE TO WRITING A BOOK 1

Chapter 1 – What Should I Write About? 3
Chapter 2 – Write 15

PART 2 – A GUIDE TO SELF-PUBLISHING A BOOK ... 23

Chapter 3 – Traditional Publishing Houses Versus Self-Publishing 25
Chapter 4 – Print Self-Publishing Books 33
Chapter 5 – Digital Self-Published Books (e-books) 53

PART 3 – A GUIDE TO MARKETING A BOOK 59

Chapter 6 – Book Marketing 101 61
Chapter 7 – Advanced Marketing Techniques 73

PART 4 – AUTHORS' TIPS 79

Chapter 8 – Common Mistakes Made In Writing,
   Self-Publishing And Marketing A Book 81
Chapter 9 – Key Points To Remember Before Writing,
   Self-Publishing And Marketing A Book 85
Chapter 10 – Useful Resources 91

CONCLUSION 95

Preface

In our attempt to self-publish and market our first three books we expended so much money, time and effort. In addition, we had printed so many copies of our print on demand books that we had to store them at home which overfilled our personal cabinets. At the time we had limited knowledge on how to effectively self-publish and market a book.

We took a few years out to gain experience from others who had self-published and marketed their books successfully. Having learnt the basics, we decided to re-edit and re-format our books, change the file covers and re-publish them. We also utilized the various self-publishing platforms, advanced marketing tools and techniques available in the market. Through the medium of the internet we now had at our disposal great resources to enable us effectively create, publish and market our books globally.

We saw our mistakes as a stepping stone on how NOT TO WRITE, SELF-PUBLISH AND MARKET A BOOK. Family, friends and colleagues who wanted to write or had written books but did not know the publishing process began to ask us questions on what they should or shouldn't do. They asked us to write a guide for them to follow. We began to research the publishing and marketing processes carefully.

Our research and study made us aware that we had missed out on some crucial steps in the process of writing, self-publishing and marketing our first three books. As we began to collate this information for them, they began to suggest that we put our knowledge into a book entitled a "simple guide" so that others can benefit from our knowledge and experience.

Anyone can write a book. It's just a matter of sitting down and writing words onto a computer or piece of paper. But, while anyone can write a book, not everyone can write a good book. And, even those who can write a good book might not know how to publish and market it. That's why this book was written. We have included some of the common mistakes that authors make; and useful tips and links. All of these combined will assist you in your quest to write, self publish and market your best-seller successfully.

Meet Tony Ramos

Tony Ramos (fictional character) is a non-fiction subject matter expert with a thriving dental practice. He wants to write a book on dentistry, self publish it, and market it to his dental practice patients. Throughout the book, we'll follow Tony as he uses the tips, strategies, and ideas that you're learning.

Your Turn

At the end of each section of the book, you'll have an opportunity to use the tips, strategies, and ideas on your own book. This way, by the end of the book, you'll have done the work you need to write, publish, and market your book.

Are you ready? Let's get started on this journey!

PART 1

A Guide To Writing A Book

Chapter 1

What Should I Write About?

Step One: Decide The Genre

One of the first questions you're going to need to answer when considering writing a book is, "What genre will my book be in?" There are two basic categories of books, fiction and non-fiction. Fiction books are stories that aren't true. Everything else is non-fiction.

Within the non-fiction category, you'll find things like business books, self-help books, cookbooks, history books, biographies and autobiographies, religion, as well as other genres such as travel books and guides, books on craft and hobbies, and science books.

Within fiction there are multiple genres and, if you intend to write creatively, you should get familiar with them and decide which one you are going to target. Perennially popular staples include romance, action and adventure, thrillers and horror whilst other, niche genres come in and out of fashion. Recent examples include vampires, werewolves and teenage magicians and, by the time you are reading this, some new fad will probably be dominating the best-sellers list!

When deciding what kind of book you want to write, you need to consider the following:

Why do I want to write a book?

Do you have some core message that you want to get out to the public? Do you want to teach your readers something? Do you want to use it as marketing for some other business you're in? Do you want to share your life story? Your purpose in writing the book is a key consideration.

Who is my audience?

Do you intend to sell the book to as many members of the general public as possible? Are you writing the book mainly for friends, family, or clients? Are you going to focus on a specific niche of readers, like dentists, mothers, or mechanics? What is the age range and reading level of your audience? Understanding your audience before you even start writing will allow you to write the book in such a way that it will appeal to the target audience.

With fiction, it is easy to fall into the trap of trying to write a book that appeals to everyone, in reality books do not often appeal to everyone. Most books will have relatively narrow markets and it is important for the author to identify what this market is and what the key factors are that these readers expect.

As an example, if you are writing for the popular Young Adult (YA) market, you will have to ensure your material appeals to the imagination of your readers whilst not being either too 'young' or babyish for them or containing 'adult' themes or language. Pitching it too 'young' will alienate your readers; too 'adult' and you will annoy their parents!

This is a hard trick to master for any genre (and particularly for YA books) and is one of the biggest reasons that authors fail to find readers – or to obtain publishing contracts and be signed up by agents if they choose to go down that route. An author needs to select a market, research it thoroughly and write for that market to achieve success.

What is my area of expertise?

One of the oldest adages in writing is write what you know. This is true for both fiction and non-fiction.

Do you have 30 years of experience in a business? Have you made a lot of money doing something? Do you have a reputation of being the best at something? Perhaps you had an unusual life experience and wish to share those lessons with your readers? It's important to write on a subject that you have some knowledge about. If you are a medical doctor and try to write a book on servicing your own automobile, you need to make sure that you have a lot of experience with cars. Otherwise, just stick to writing about medicine.

With fiction, particularly when you are starting out, it is often best to write about things that are within your experience and knowledge. It is hard to write about Special Forces combat in Afghanistan with believable authority if you are a retired postmistress who has never ventured much further than your local seaside resort[1]. With practice this might be possible but, at first, your writing will only convince others if you are writing about what you know perhaps with your characters based upon people you know (though be very careful about this; these people might recognise themselves and not like what you have done with them!).

---

[1] Hard but not impossible! That is the beauty of writing fiction; with enough research and a good enough style, a good writer convinces the reader that he/she DOES know what they are telling them

If our postmistress starts to write stories about where she lives and the people she has met, perhaps spinning new storylines that might involve secrets, lies and suburban murders all hidden behind the lace curtains then she is likely to convince her readers that the world she has created is real and she would well be on her way to a sales success.

How strong a writer am I?

If you are a terrible speller, don't know a preposition from a pronoun, and break out into a cold sweat at the thought of writing a book alone, consider working with a writing expert. Many writers collaborate with others to help fill gaps in their writing skill set. Even if you are a strong writer, you should be sure and have your book professionally edited. Even bestselling authors tend to miss their own mistakes and spell check is famously unreliable.

You should be aware that there are a number of different people involved with book production and you should ensure that, if you are going to employ someone to help you, you know what their skills are. A proofreader will only check for errors in spelling and grammar and spot missing passages. An editor (or copy-editor) will go deeper and will often suggest deeper changes that will improve a book. There are also writing coaches and consultants who will advise you on your manuscript – for a fee.

Be cautious; these services can be expensive and there are many people out there who will charge expensive fees for work of a dubious quality. If you are employing someone, check that they have a recognised qualification or they are a member of a recognised trade association.

Places which offer training for editors and proofreaders can be found at the following websites:

> http://www.train4publishing.co.uk/
> http://www.chapterhousepublishing.co.uk/
> http://www.the-efa.org/eve/education.php

What do I hope to achieve with this book?

Non-fiction

Goals for writing and publishing your book may include establishing your expertise in a particular field. Having a successful book published is a very good way of marketing yourself, your services or your business. This is also a good reason why your book should be as good as it possibly can be; if this is your motivation it is vitally important that the book makes the right impression.

Other non-fiction writers are trying to make a difference – saving the environment, promoting good or important causes, drawing society's attention to something that they may have overlooked or disregarded. The goal here is to get the point across in the most effective and lucid way possible, showing others why the cause is important and why it needs their attention.

Finally, some people just do it for the fame and satisfaction of seeing a book with their name on it in print. There is nothing wrong with this at all; it is certainly a thrill to hold a book with your name on the spine. It is a great achievement.

Fiction

Many fiction writers entertain hopes of writing the next global blockbuster that will make them Millionaires. It CAN happen but, like entering the lottery or a TV talent contest, for the vast majority it will end in disappointment. There are tens of thousands of novels written each year, many thousands are published but only a select few sell in quantities.

Don't' however be put off by this; as long as your goals are realistic, you can have a very satisfying and fulfilling writing career. If, for example, you write a novel that hundreds of people enjoy, which makes someone laugh or cry or contact a long lost relative because of what you have written, isn't that an achievement?

Success in writing fiction does not have to be measured in the number of sales you have made. Your writing can take you to places, worlds and situations that would otherwise be closed to you. Many writers simply enjoy the process of world creation and storytelling. Just immersing yourself in the world you have created can be rewarding enough; sales success is a bonus.

Writing can be one of the most satisfying creative practices you can do and, unlike painting or calligraphy where the ability to share or sell your work is limited, there is the medium and technology now that can deliver your work to customers.

Now that you've answered these questions, it's now time to move on to the next step in writing your book. But first, let's see how Tony Ramos implemented Step One.

Tony Ramos

Why do I want to write a book?

I developed a new flossing technique that I want to share with my patients and the general dental public.

Who is my audience?

Adults who still have their natural teeth

What is my area of expertise?

I am a dentist and have been using my method for 20 years in my own practice.

How strong a writer am I?

I'm a pretty good writer. I believe I can write the book myself and simply have it edited when I'm done.

Your Turn

Why do I want to write a book?

Who is my audience?

What is my area of expertise?

How strong a writer am I?

Step Two: Research Your Topic

Researching for a non-fiction book

You might be thinking, "I am a subject matter expert. I don't need to do any research on my topic!" But this isn't true. It's always a good idea to do some research on your topic—even if it's your own autobiography! When you acknowledge resources used in your book, it adds credibility and provides additional information and value to your readers. Here are some things to keep in mind when researching your topic.

Who are the other experts on my topic? Ideally your book will present the ideas, thoughts, or methods of the other experts and then make them better or challenge them in some way.

How can you research your topic? First, talk to your friends, family, associates, or the organisations in your subject. If you're writing your autobiography, talk to your relatives to see how they remember things. If you're writing about classic cars, post a message to a message board asking relevant questions.

Do some Internet research. Enter some key words into a search engine and see what comes up. Be careful, though, that you use reliable sources and don't copy anyone else's work. But, sites like Google Scholar can help you locate some credible information on your topic.

Visit the library and check out other books on your subject. Again, don't copy anyone's ideas, but you can mention the other key authors, theories, and information in your book as long as you cite the source and give a reference. Don't include any photographs, charts, or long passages of text without written permission. That's copyright infringement and you don't want to do that.

Researching for a Fiction Book

You may be surprised to see this heading – research for fiction? Surely that's not necessary, fiction is all made up.

Research in fiction is usually essential. Some of the most popular and successful fiction is so because the background it takes place against is convincing. This is only achieved by impeccable research. Authors who are renowned for this include John LeCarré in his espionage novels, Frederick Forsyth for his thrillers and Robert Harris whose novels such as Enigma, Pompeii and Imperium all take place in real historical settings. Their work is a success because the worlds that their largely fictional characters inhabit convince the reader that this is how they really are or were. This does not happen by accident; it comes about by way of a lot of research.

Rules/Conventions of Fiction Even when you are creating entirely fictional worlds such as you might do if writing fantasy or Sci Fi there are usually 'rules' or 'conventions' that you have to understand and follow. For example, everyone just 'knows' that vampires hate daylight and that werewolves only change form during the full moon. Even if these beings are entirely fictional and generally accepted as such. Yet these rules are still valid nonetheless and if, in your novel or short story, you have a vampire who sunbathes or werewolves who can change form whenever they want then you will have some very puzzled readers.

The rule is do your research carefully so your worlds – even if they are the product of your imagination – appear as 'real' as possible.

Let's see how Tony researched his topic.

Tony Ramos

Since Tony invented a new technique for flossing, he did some research on the history of floss, the types of flosses available, and the current best practices on flossing. He included some statistics on gum disease and how flossing can prevent it. He also cited some of the other books on dental care.

Tony also talked to his clients and discussed his book with a couple of his dentist friends over a game of golf. He wanted their input into the kinds of things they'd want to read in a book on flossing.

Your Turn

Take a piece of paper or use your computer to list the ways you'll research your topic.

Chapter 2

Write

Step Three: Start Writing

Having a blank page staring back at you can be one of the most intimidating things about writing. There are many ways that you can go about starting the process of writing. Some authors prefer to create an outline and work from that. Others use a brainstorming or a "mind dump" process where they get everything they want to say down on paper before they organize it. Here are some tips you can use to start writing your book.

Develop a plan.

Whether you're working from an outline or plan to just brainstorm, develop a plan for how you're going to write the book. The most important first step in writing is to decide in advance how you will approach the book.

With a non-fiction, factual book, you may be able to define all of the sections it will have to contain; creating the section headings will show you exactly what you have got to write. It also gives you the opportunity to write non-sequentially, filling in the gaps of the sections where you have lots of information and leaving the more difficult sections until later. This is a great way of making progress.

With a fiction book, planning varies. Some writers do not plan at all but let the story 'develop'; personal experience tells us that it is these books that often do not get finished! Many writers have a loose overall outline of what the book is about, who the characters are and, ideally, how it ends. Some go no further than this plan, others do periodic 'section' plans that outline how the plot develops and which events and character interactions have to take place to advance the novel.

This planning is rather looser than what happens with a non-fiction book, giving the author flexibility to develop plot ideas and characters as the book develops but encouraging progress and giving a definite goal; the ending. How much you plan depends on you as an individual but it is recommended that you do some degree of planning as this will definitely help you make progress.

Choose the structure for the book.

How many chapters will it have? Will you divide it into parts? Do you want to get someone to write a Foreword for you?

Look at other books you like.

Go to Amazon.com or another online bookstore and take a look inside some of the other books on the market. See what contents they included and how they approached their topics. Of course, you're not looking at it to copy it. You simply want to see how the other authors approached their books and get some inspiration for writing your own.

Choose a specific time to write.

Some authors like to write for an hour or two in the morning. Others write every night. Some have to do it on the weekends, when the kids are asleep, or find some other way to fit writing into their schedule. Whichever time you choose, make sure that you pick a time that will work regularly and then stick to it. This is the single most effective thing you can do to advance your book.

Don't worry about coming up with the perfect title or the perfect first line.

Just start writing. After the first couple of paragraphs, things will start to flow. After all, this book has probably been in your head for a long time. Just sit down, start writing, and let it out. You'll revise later.

Don't be tempted by distractions.

It's very easy to lose your focus when you're writing. A text message will come in, you'll want to check Facebook, take a nap, or go to the kitchen for a snack. Don't! Stay focused. This is why you need to have a structure and a specific time and place. It helps keep you focused.

One little trick that we employ is, when we are coming to the end of a writing session, is to leave the section that we are working on unfinished. This may seem odd but one of the big problems when *starting* a new writing session is the motivation, putting words down and getting into the flow of writing. If you are starting a new session this can be hard but if you start knowing what you have to write – as you do when you have unfinished work from the previous session – you are getting over that hurdle straight away and should be in a good writing rhythm by the time you get to the new bit.

Get an accountability partner.

Ask someone to hold you accountable for your writing. Send them your chapters as you finish them or find some other way to let your partner know that you're on track. There are writing coaches who can provide this support (as well as feedback on the quality of your work). But, you don't have to hire a pro. Just a friend or family member who is willing to hold you accountable is sufficient.

Join a writing group

A good writing group, whether it is one that sets little writing exercises or one that you read out work-in-progress to for a critique, is invaluable, particularly for creative writing. Writing can be a lonely business; a group can give you encouragement and support. It also will sharpen your writing skills; members spot errors, cliché ridden, stodgy prose and will suggest improvements. They are also great for sparking ideas for new projects.

Search on the internet or ask in your local library for your closest group. If there isn't one, why not start one yourself!

Stay motivated.

There are lots of resources to help you stay motivated when writing. Writer's Digest, WriteorDie.com, and onetwofiver.com are good sites to help you blast through any writer's block.

Also, make sure that your book has the expected elements of a professionally written book. These include a title, copyright notice, introduction, main body, illustrations, and an index.

Once you've completed your rough draft of your book, take a few days off and come back and polish it. Get someone else to read the book (not someone who'll just tell you it's great, but someone who will offer constructive feedback) and then go back and make revisions.

Step Four: Edit

Trying to edit one's own work is a lot like looking at your own child. You can't really see the flaws as well as someone from the outside . . . When you write, rewrite, revise, and rework your book numerous times, your eyes tend to glaze over even some of the more obvious errors. There are many kinds of errors that spell check will miss. It's always a good idea to have your book professionally edited.

Here are two resources for places to go to hire a reasonably priced copyeditor:

>   www.elance.com
>   www.guru.com

Even if you don't choose to use a professional copyeditor, there are some things you can do to make sure that your book is as "clean" as possible. **Here are some tips from self-publishing company iUniverse:**

Check for spelling consistency.

There is often more than one way to spell a word. For example, copy editing, copy-editing, and copyediting are all technically correct. When you choose a specific spelling of a word, make sure that you use the same one throughout your manuscript. Also make sure that if you are using British, Canadian, Australian, or American English that you keep the spelling consistent as well.

Check your abbreviations.

Similar to spelling, there are many correct ways to abbreviate words—I.T. versus IT for example. Make sure you are consistent throughout.

Check your bullet lists.

Use the same kind of bullet points, the same syntax, and the same punctuation in each.

Check your facts.

Be sure and use properly presented references and documentation for the facts and information you use. IUniverse uses The Chicago Manual of Style format for references. No matter what style you use, make sure that you use references and that they are formatted correctly.

Let's see how Tony is doing:

Tony Ramos

Tony decided to work on an outline. He developed a schedule that he would block off two hours on Mondays, Wednesdays, and Fridays during lunch at the office (when the receptionist and hygienists were taking lunch and doing paperwork) to write. The first writing session was a bit intimidating for Tony as he sat staring at a blank computer screen. But, he'd promised his brother Johnny that he would get him a rough outline by the end of the day. So, Tony went over to Amazon.com and searched for other books written by dentists. He got inspired and created his outline in two hours!

Over the next three months, Tony diligently worked during his scheduled writing time, finished his rough draft, had a dentist friend of his read it, revised it, and sent it off to be professionally edited. Tony was so proud that he'd written his first book!

Your Turn

In the following space, develop your plan for writing your book. When will you write? What would you write? How will you stay motivated? How will you avoid distractions?

Okay, now you've read this chapter. Put the book down and start writing your own book!

PART 2

A Guide To Self-Publishing A Book

Chapter 3

Traditional Publishing Houses Versus Self–Publishing

Now that you have got a completed manuscript, it's time to publish it! There are two basic ways to go about this – traditional publishing houses or some form of self-publishing.

Traditional Publishing Houses

What are traditional publishing houses?

In today's digital world it is getting increasingly hard to generalise about publishing but, basically, traditional publishing houses are companies who commission, edit and issue books, both in traditional print and electronically, from and on behalf of the author. They do everything for the author including organising proofreading, copy-editing and undertaking the promotion and marketing of the book, ensuring it gets into all of the suitable sales outlets.

In exchange for their input, they take the majority of the receipts for the book, the author being left with between 10-20% as royalties from which they have to pay their agent's commission. This may seem an unfair division of money however the publisher is the one taking on the risk by investing considerable time and money in the book – producing and marketing a book professionally is an expensive business.

Non-fiction books—the leading publishers include Pearson, Reed Elsevier, Thomson Reuters, Wolters Kluwer, Hachette Livre, Grupo Planeta and McGraw-Hill Education. These publishers have imprints that serve the professions – Law, Medicine, Accountancy, Property/Real Estate etc. – as well producing more general, mass market appeal non-fiction titles.

Fiction books—there are a few giants of the publishing world (including some of the above), the big six generally taken to be Hachette, Harpercollins, Macmillan, Penguin group, Random House and Simon & Schuster. All of these publishing houses issue books under their parent label but also have smaller, often more specialised publishing companies with their group[2]

There are also a lot of smaller, independent publishers who often publish in specialised, niche areas – genres such as sci fi or fantasy, or serve certain groups of authors – Virago who solely publishes books written by women or those who publish in certain regions only – specialist Scottish and Irish Publishers. These publishers only produce a few books a year but are often more approachable than the traditional giants. There are also some small publishers who

---

[2] Penguin, for example, include Ace Books, Alpha Books, Amy Einhorn Books/Putnam, Avery, Berkley Books, Dial Books for Young Readers, Dutton Books, Dutton Children's Books, Firebird, Frederick Warne, Gotham Books, G.P. Putnam's Sons, G.P. Putnam's Sons Books for Young Readers, Grosset & Dunlap, HP Books, Hudson Street Press, Jove, NAL, Pamela Dorman Books, Penguin, The Penguin Press, Perigee Books, Philomel Books, Plume, Portfolio, Prentice Hall Press, Price Stern Sloan, Puffin Books, Razorbill, Riverhead, Sentinel, Speak, Tarcher and The Viking Press, Viking Books for Young Readers within their group

produce only e-books therefore saving themselves the printing costs and utilising mainly web-based marketing routes for promoting their authors. It is a grey area as to whether the latter do much more than a good independent author can do for themselves.

Finally there are certain types of publishers which should be avoided. These are the ones who require you to pay all or part of the publishing costs, the latter being marketed as 'Joint Venture' publishing. These companies market themselves extensively on the web and in writing magazines. Their primary purpose is to make money but, unlike the mainstream publishers, tend to do this from their authors rather than from sales of the books. They may charge for services such as editing and proofreading and invariably for 'promotional packages' to push your book in book fairs and the like. Anecdotal evidence suggests that very few authors gain sales higher than the costs that they have expended.

If you have chosen to go down this route but are having doubts, you can find out what other people are saying about them. You can check out other people's comments at the following links **http:// www.sfwa.org/for-authors/writer-beware/alerts/** and **http:// webnews.sff.net/**, both of which have archives of warnings and messages about what their contributors feel are scam operations.

For lists of publishers you may check the Writers and Artists Yearbook at the following website: **http://www.writersandartists. co.uk**) or websites such as **www.firstwriter.com**, both of which have up-to-date lists of agents and publishers from all around the world. They also have other useful information such as the contact details and requirements of magazine and periodicals that publish new materials, as well as information on writing competitions.

Pros of traditional publishing houses

If you are lucky enough to get in with a professional publisher you have the advantage of having them on board with YOU as a stakeholder in the success of your book. Publishers are not in business for charity; they will do everything to try to ensure that your book is a success. They will appoint an editor to work with you and a proofreader (usually a freelancer) to check the material over. They will create a marketing programme for you and will promote your book before it is launched. Publishers have good contacts with booksellers and will aim to place your book in all suitable sales outlets at a realistic price.

Cons of traditional publishing houses

When a book is traditionally published, the publishing house exerts control over every step of the process. Although you, as author, produce the text and have a say in the final content, everything else falls under the control of the publisher. It is analogous to the difference between being self-employed and working for someone; the latter gives you a lot of security, you just do what you are supposed to do and, in time, you will get paid, however you have to abide by the rules and, ultimately, do what your employer says or leave. You lose that overall control and freedom that you had when you were just the author with a book idea.

And, of course, you will lose the majority of the proceeds from selling your book. Of the net receipts expect to get only 10-20% of the total if you are the sole author – and a share of this if you have shared the writing duties!

There are other difficulties with working with a traditional publishing house. One is the pace at which it works. From commissioning a book, through writing and the production process to seeing the finished product on the shelves can easily take

18-24 months. It is a slow, methodical process. This can suit you if this is your life's work that you are writing about and want to do justice to it or you are an academic producing a new textbook but it is frustrating if you want to get fresh ideas in front of a new audience as soon as possible. If, for example, you are writing a book to promote your business, taking the slow route of traditional publishing may not be for you.

In addition, if you are a non-fiction writer with no track record of writing or publication, you may find it difficult to get a publisher to take you on. The reason is simple; sales potential. If you write a recipe book, for example, based on the delicious recipes of your mother or grandmother, it really does not matter how good the food tastes; you are going up against all of the celebrity chefs whose works sell in the thousands simply because of their name. It is unlikely that the publisher would take you on as they know they would struggle to sell your title.

In fiction, things are more difficult. For a start, as a new author, you cannot take a few chapters of a partly completed work to a publisher; they would reject you immediately. You will have to have a completed manuscript that is thoroughly checked and has been redrafted several times. Even then it is unlikely that a big publisher would bother to read it; they generally only read work that has been supplied to them by recognised literary agents because they know that the latter will have filtered out weak submissions and will only send them the best.

So, to ensure success, you will need to be taken on by a literary agent first. And here is another difficulty because the vast majority of agents are extremely busy and only take on a handful of new clients each year. A literary agent makes a living by taking 10-15% of their clients' earnings per year so they will only take on clients that have the potential to sell a lot of books.

There are many thousands of books written each year, and many find themselves on the 'slush piles' of literary agents, some get read whilst most get rejected. Getting a literary agent is an essential step to getting published traditionally however the vast majority of authors will fail to achieve this.

This is one of the reasons why the self-publishing route has proved so popular.

Self-Publishing

What is self-publishing?

Self-publishing is the term given to anything published directly by the author themselves.

Self-publishing used to have a certain stigma attached to it. One branch of self-publishing was called 'vanity publishing' where an author would pay anything from several hundred to many thousands of $/£/Euros to produce a limited print run of their books in order, usually, simply to see their name in print. These books, either fiction or non-fiction, had varied production quality ranging from shoddy to professional, and the content was often poor.

Those days have largely gone. Publishing has been revolutionised and democratised by technology in much the same way that YouTube has enabled some talented amateur filmmakers, news and musical artists to present their material to a wide audience without the intervention of TV and Movie companies. It is now relatively easy for anyone and everyone to publish, either electronically through Amazon's ubiquitous Kindle platform, or on Kobo, Nook, Sony e-reader or one of the other e-reader applications, or in print form through the Print-On-Demand (POD) services such as CreateSpace, Lulu and Lightening Source (LSI).

The standard can still be uneven but there are some very good quality works that have been self-published. This movement has shocked the rather staid world of traditional publishing; indeed the industry is struggling to come to terms with its implications.

Oddly, the self-publishing movement may, in fact, make it more difficult for writers to be published conventionally, as revenue is diverted away from the traditional book purchase to e-published material, small publishers in particular, who do not have the 'bankers' of big name authors in their catalogue, are struggling financially and may not be available for authors in the future.

Pros of self-publishing

There are a number of advantages to self-publishing. For a start, many of the barriers that exist in traditional publishing that prevent many quality books from being produced are removed. You are in total control of the process – and will receive the majority of the receipts. Amazon's Kindle, for example, have two royalty options, one giving you 35% and one 70% of the receipts (the former allows you to set lower prices that may be good for driving sales; the latter is restricted to certain countries). The process is also much quicker; important if you are likely to use your book to promote yourself or an aspect of your business.

As we will see later, the process of self-publishing is now quite easy and, with care (and a little effort), producing a professional standard book you can be proud of is within the reach of everyone.

Cons of self-publishing

There are some downsides to self-publishing. Firstly, there is a degree of residual stigma from the old vanity publishing days that still affects people's views of self-published books. It is likely that gradually this will fade away.

Other issues will always be there, however. The author has to do all of the production process for themselves – proofing, editing, deciding on the layout, page sizing, colours etc., as well as design or commissioning a cover design. This can be quite daunting and may require skillsets that the author may not have.

In addition, the author has to do all of the promotion and marketing for themselves – and this can be quite difficult. However, just as technology has opened up the possibilities of self-publishing itself, it also offers many routes to the self-published author to create shop-windows for themselves.

After we have guided you through the mechanics of producing a book, we will cover how you can market your book to maximise its sales potential.

Chapter 4

Print Self-Publishing Books

We are going to focus on self-publishing in this Book. This chapter focuses on publishing a paper book. In the next chapter, we would look at digital publishing.

Why self-publish?

The main reason an author would want to self-publish his or her book is that it allows for exclusive creative control over the book. You might be told to edit the title, change the content, shorten or lengthen the book, or to make some other kind of change that you don't want to make. When you self-publish, you maintain control.

Also, it's possible to retain a greater percentage of the profit when you self publish. Traditional publishers generally offer a 20% royalty to authors. With some self-publishing options, you can retain 50-100% of the profit.

It used to be that the advantage of traditional publishing was that the author would often get a large advance, a sponsored book tour, and extensive marketing. Because traditional publishing houses have taken a financial hit due to the proliferation of self-publishing options, this is no longer the case. Unless you are already famous, you're going to have to do as much marketing of your traditionally published book as you would a self-published one. So, why not maintain editorial control and greater royalties by publishing yourself?

Self-Publishing Options

There are three core ways one can go about self-publishing a paper book namely:

- have the books printed yourself
- go with a print-on-demand publisher who will do many of the functions that a conventional publisher will do
- do the full self production entirely yourself using companies like CreateSpace, Lulu.com or LSI.

Frankly, printing physical books yourself is a major hassle. You've got to pay in advance to have them printed, find a place to store them, and then physically pack, label, post, and ship each order.

Instead, a simpler option is to use one of the many print-on-demand companies. Print-on-demand works this way. You find a company that has a package that you like. Fees range from free to several thousand dollars. You pay the fee (if applicable), upload your manuscript electronically, the company can design a cover for you, will typeset the book, bind it, and will print and ship each copy for you. Generally, you'll get one or more free copies of your own book. These companies often have additional services which you can purchase for a fee such as copyediting, book reviews, marketing services etc.

Many of these print-on-demand companies will assign your book an ISBN number (the International Standard Book Number, which is the identification number for your book), and will offer it for sale to online retailers such as Amazon.com and Barnes and Noble.

The advantages of using print-on-demand for your paper books are numerous.

Some of the advantages are obvious; you can get a very professional looking result without having to go to the expense of commissioning a print run. POD is exactly that; you print on DEMAND when you actually need copies and you only need to order the amount you think you might need. Another advantage is that you can quickly make adjustments to your text or bring out special editions for special events – a training course, a promotional or charity event. This would be impossible with conventionally published books.

There are some disadvantages, though. Some of which are –

First, because you are uploading your own manuscript file, the book will be printed exactly as you upload it. If there are spelling errors or other mistakes, they will show up in your book.

Also, your book will not be sold in physical bookstores unless you specifically contact them to arrange for that (although Amazon's CreateSpace POD company does allow you to purchase additional marketing channels which include being listed on physical bookshop's inventories).

Finally, as mentioned, you'll need to do all of your own marketing. Book signings, videos and posters which all cost additional money.

The following are some of the places where you can go to self-publish your book:

    LULU.com
    CreateSpace
    Lightning Source (LSI)
    Author Solutions
    Niche publishers

Westbow
Dellarte Press
Kindle Direct Publishing

Things to Consider when choosing where to publish:

When deciding where to publish your book you will need to consider the following items (please note that these items vary from publisher to publisher):

Author Support:

Does the company have someone within the publishing house that will offer you guidance and support throughout the process? The big self-publishing companies normally give you two levels of support; one is do-it-yourself, often step-by-step guidance taking you through to publication, whilst the second option is professional, personal assistance which you will have to pay for.

Rights:

Do you maintain full rights to your work? It's important that you choose a company that will allow you to maintain the rights to your work. You want to be able to publish it elsewhere at a later date if you wish.

Copyright/ISBN:

Does the company register the copyright for you? Give you an ISBN number? (The International Standard Book Number (ISBN) is a unique 13 digit (from 2007, prior to this they had 10 digits) numeric commercial book identifier, tied to a barcode. Each section of the ISBN gives information about the book – its group or type, publisher identifier, title number and check digit.)

Cover Design:

Do you need someone to design your cover for you? Most of the places have cover design services available. These can either be basic covers held within the system which are free or a premium design service for which you will be charged.

Free Author Books:

Do you receive a free author copy of your book? How many?

Images:

How many images are allowed in the book? Can you include colour photos or only black and white?

Editorial Support:

Does the company offer editing services? If so, which ones and at what cost?

Marketing Support:

What marketing services does the company offer?

Sales Channels:

Where is the book offered for sale? Is it only on the publishing house's website, or can customers buy it from Amazon.com and Barnes and Noble.com?

Steps for Self Publishing Your Book

Okay, now that you understand the basics, here are the steps to follow to publish your book. It should be noted that authors reviews show that CreateSpace, Lightning Source and LULU as the main three self-publishing platforms preferred in the market. (We would go into more detail about their specific requirements later in this chapter)

1: **Choose your publisher.**

Ensure that any editorial and formatting services that you plan to do is completed before choosing a Publisher. Once the book is ready chose your publisher before moving on to the next step.

2: **Carefully follow their instructions for formatting the file.**

Some companies (Create Space, for example) have VERY specific instructions for embedding fonts and formatting. If you don't follow the instructions exactly, your book won't look right. If you're concerned about your ability to do this, consider using a company like The Fast Fingers.com who can format your book for you, they can be found at **http://www.thefastfingers.com**.

3. **Get an ISBN number.**

If the publisher you chose doesn't give you one, you will have to get an ISBN number yourself. ISBNs are assigned to Publishers in the country where the Publisher's main office is based. This is irrespective of the language of the publication or the intended market for the book. Each Country has its own National Agency responsible for awarding ISBNs to publishers and self-publishers within their country and territories. For example the USA would not assign ISBNs to publishers and self-publishers located outside the USA and its territories (most countries abide by the same rule).

As a Self-Publisher you will have to approach the relevant Agency in the country where you reside. Nielsenbook is the National Agency for the assignment of ISBNs in the UK and Republic of Ireland see **http://www.isbn.nielsenbook.co.uk/** whilst Bowker is the ISBN Agency in the USA, see **http://www.isbn.org/standards/home/index.asp**.

In order to find the Agency responsible for assigning ISBNs in the country in which you are resident you should refer to the following International ISBN Agency's website which provides agencies for nearly all the countries in the world **http://www.isbn-international.org/agency**.

You should note that there is no legal requirement to have an ISBN for a published book in most countries, however should you wish to sell your publication through internet booksellers and major publishing companies they would ask you to provide an ISBN.

4. Upload your book.

To upload your manuscript and files covers follow the instruction given by the publisher.

5. Approve the book cover.

If you didn't design the cover yourself and are having the publisher design it for you, you'll need to approve the cover prior to publication. Depending on the level of customer service provided by the publisher you chose, you can request a redesign. Note that most of the POD allow you to import your own cover as long as it conforms to their template. There are a number of freelance book cover designers available on freelancer site such as Elance.com and PeoplePerHour.com who can design you covers at a very reasonable rate and most will be familiar with the processes required for POD publishing and will be able to guide you as to what is required.

6. **Proof the print version of the book.**

Before final publication, you'll have an opportunity to proof the final book. On many sites you have the option of looking at an electronic facsimile of the completed book, down loading a PDF image of the book in its print format which you can print out or give you the option of ordering print proofs at a discounted cost.

Be meticulous in looking for errors as, once it's published, you'll need to pay again (if you've chosen a publisher that requires payment) to fix any errors after publication. Look for things like typos, hanging headers, graphics that run onto the next page, font size inconsistencies, and things like this.

7. **Approve the final book.**

Now that you've done everything you can and have approved the book, it will only take a few days for your book to be available for sale. Your author copies should be in your hands within a week to ten days.

Let us now focus on the particular requirements and Steps to self-publish your book at CreateSpace, Lulu and Lightning Source and why choose any of these platforms to self-publish your manuscript.

You will find that all 3 platforms have their own specifications and requirements which you must comply with to the letter.

CreateSpace

The CreateSpace process is examined here in some detail as CreateSpace is becoming the most common route to publication (although Lulu.com claims that 1 million authors have used their services as at the beginning of 2013).

a. Why choose CreateSpace as a platform to publish your book:

The big advantage (or disadvantage depending upon your viewpoint as some people dislike Amazon and their way of doing business) is that CreateSpace is part of the Amazon empire. Publishing with CreateSpace, even using the free distribution channels (see below) will get your book listed on the Amazon websites all over the world. Buying the extended distribution channels will give you the opportunity to be listed outside the Amazon system including being placed on the lists of conventional bookshops. The CreateSpace process also goes a long way towards preparing your book for publication on Kindle, though the operation is often not as seamless as you might imagine.

Another advantage of CreateSpace in our experience is the cost; CreateSpace seems to consistently produce the lowest unit costs. Their cost per unit was at least 25% below that of the next cheapest, Lulu.com. The self-publishing world is very competitive; therefore this price advantage may change over time.

b. Requirements for Self-Publishing at CreateSpace

CreateSpace supports documents in print-ready PDF, .doc, .docx and RTF formats[3]

---

[3] For those who might be wondering exactly what these are we will provide an explanation here, PDF is Adobe's Portable Document Format, a cross-platform, format stable way of presenting documents. Print ready refers to the way the manuscript has been saved. The two doc suffixes, .doc and .docx are Microsoft Word files, the former the old version, the latter the version in Word 2007 onward. Many free Office clone programmes like Open Office and Libre Office allow saves in either .doc or .docx format (and PDF too). RTF stands for Rich Text Format and is Microsoft's cross-platform system. All Word versions and the free office clones allow saves in RTF format.

c. Steps for Self Publishing Your Book at Create Space

If you select CreateSpace as your publishing platform you will have to create an account with them. The process is simple; you will require just an email address and a password. You can go through the entire process and not take the final step to publication by 'holding' the process at the review stage. Some authors choose to do this if they have a manuscript that is with a publisher for consideration for professional publication; it also gives the author a chance to order review copies of the completed book for family and friends, for publicity or for special events without committing to publication.

When you register with CreateSpace for publication you are given the option to do the entire process yourself or to use some or all of the paid services offered by the company. If you choose to do-it-yourself there are two options available; a guided route for people that have not been through the process before, or an 'expert' route for those who are used to it. The step-by-step guide covered here is the guided option.

The first screen once this route is selected is one where you give the title of the book, its author or authors, contributors, the series title if it is part of a suite of other books, its language and publication date. This latter item can be left blank; a publication date will automatically be assigned when the book goes 'live' on sale.

Note that it is important to be as accurate and complete as possible with this information as once an ISBN number has been allocated this information is fixed.

The ISBN allocation is on the next screen. An ISBN can be allocated free by CreateSpace or you can obtain your own (there are links on the screen to do so). Note, once an ISBN number has been allocated to a title it cannot be changed.

The next step is to decide on the interior type – whether the book is to be printed in black and white or colour and the paper to be white or cream. Obviously, black and white printing on white paper produces the lowest cost.

Immediately after choosing the interior type you choose the trim size. This is essentially the size of your book. The most common size of book you will see is the size most paperbacks come in: 6 x 9 format (15.24 x 22.86 cm) and this tends to be the cheapest option, however you must choose the format that best fits your book. If, for example, you are producing a business type book with, say, a number of complex spreadsheet examples, you will need a larger trim size so that the readers can see the figures more easily.

One thing to note is that CreateSpace has templates for documents suitable for all their trim sizes. They come in two forms; either a blank one that will just allocate your text to the correct space on the page size selected and a fully formatted template containing things like copyright notices and an index which you paste your text into. It is very useful to use these as the default settings on most Word packages is an A4 size (29.7 x 21.0 cm, 11.7 x 8.3 in), i.e. considerably bigger than the 6 x 9 trim. Shrinking an A4 page directly onto this page size is going to give a very odd looking result; your text will need repaginating. Even if you do not use the full template it is worth looking at it as it will give a guide as to what is expected from a book to give it a professional look and feel.

The next step is to upload the interior in one of the forms that CreateSpace require – PDF, doc, docx or RTF as discussed above.

Print Ready PDF – an explanation

Most people are familiar with PDF documents. PDF was created by Adobe in the early days of personal computers to give a cross-platform way of sending and receiving documents. It has continued to prove useful and many print and e-books use PDFs as their preferred text source.

However you must use the right type of PDF! What you need is a print ready PDF with embedded fonts. Most word processing packages have a PDF print option however this is not the type of PDF you need. In later versions of Word you need to go through the file save options and set up to be a PDF/A—1a format on export. In programmes like Libre office there is an export to PDF button on the toolbar however you need to use the File – Export as PDF menu option to allow you to set up the PDF export as follows:

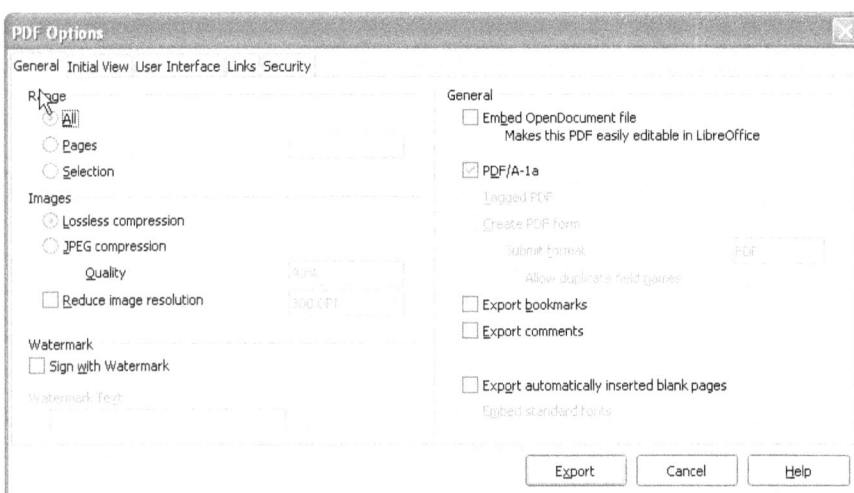

Note the requirement to move the type to Lossless compression as well.

The PDF files produced will then be suitable for use by most of the POD publishing companies.

Once downloaded there is an automatic check carried out by the system which will pick up any formatting problems, minor spelling mistakes and problems with the resolution of any images that you have put into text. Later, once you have completed the cover creator step and saved the files, the full package is reviewed by the CreateSpace team. This can take up to 12 hours and is to check for suitability and legality of what is submitted.

Before getting to this step, however, you need to create a cover for the book. There are three options that you can use for this; either you can upload your own cover, using a template that CreateSpace supply, or you can use the company's own design service (at a cost) or you can use build-a-cover function which is a DIY option. We will use the latter here.

There are 30 different templates that can be selected. Once you have chosen one each is customisable for colour, font and layout. Once you have chosen your template you build it step-by-step adding photographs, cover blurb, author biography and photograph if required. This process has to be completed before you move on to final publication but can be left and saved so you can return to it later.

Once this is completed the files go off to CreateSpace for review. Once this step is taken you have the opportunity to work through a proof. There are three options here; there is a very good virtual image that you can use to do an on-screen check. You can download a PDF version either to be printed out or checked on screen or you can order a physical proof copy of your book. This comes from the US. If you are outside the US this can mean that it can take 2-3 weeks to receive a copy or else you can pay for more rapid delivery (2-3 days) at a premium cost. Note, once you have approved the proof with every other step completed, including the ones below, then the book is officially published and available.

The next stages before publication are the distribution options, pricing and description stages.

With distribution, you have the option of just selling through Amazon, or else paying a small premium (at the time of writing US$25) to have wider distribution channels. This includes bookstores and online retailers outside Amazon and libraries and academic institutions – the latter possibly being important to non-fiction writers.

The starting point for the price calculation is the calculated production costs for the book. This is the minimum price that CreateSpace will allow you to sell the book for. As noted above, our experience is that CreateSpace is around 25% cheaper than the main POD alternatives, but this may change over time. The price set for sale in the US (CreateSpace is, after all, an American company) can be used to set the price for the other country specific Amazon sites or you can set any price for these markets as long as it is above the minimum price set by the system that is based on the production costs.

The description of the book is more than the back cover blurb – although you can use this here if you want. This is the opportunity to be more expansive about what is in the book. It is also the place where you set the BISAC category (Book Industry Standards and Communication Categories). This is the code that booksellers use to identify and group books according to their subject matter so is essential if you want to sell the book widely. You can either enter the code if you know it or build it up from a drop-down menu of descriptions.

At the end of this section is a place for entering keywords. This is for use for search engines so should be done as carefully and accurately as possible.

Once you have completed the process and had the content and cover approved by CreateSpace you are then ready to publish.

The CreateSpace process is very easy and largely foolproof. It also resembles the processes that are used in the other two systems described below, so we will cover these in slightly less detail.

LULU

a. Why choose Lulu as a platform to publish your book:

Lulu.com offer a similar range of services to CreateSpace, i.e. either a full DIY option or a series of packaged services ranging from help with individual elements including cover design, illustrations, editing, publicity and promotion all the way to a full publication package.

Lulu is also one of the oldest of the POD operations and claim that over 1 million authors have used their services up to the beginning of 2013. Lulu also provides a service to publish e-books in a cross-platform i-bookstore and Nook form (but not Kindle).

b. Requirements for Self-Publishing at Lulu

Lulu supports a wide range of text including Word (.doc and .docx), RTF, Google Docs, Open Office, Libre Office and Apple Pages. However, it does prefer the document to be in print ready PDF format (see above).

c. Steps for Self Publishing Your Book at Lulu

The steps needed to publish are quite similar to that of CreateSpace. On registration with Lulu (using a valid e-mail address and a password – you have to validate your e-mail before you can publish) you can choose to keep the project private or select a sales option. If you offer it in bookshops then an ISBN number is allocated to it.

You then enter the title, paper type, trim size, binding type (you can use more options here than CreateSpace including a spiral bound option useful for business workbooks and Lulu also offer a hardback option) and colour or B&W options.

Once this is all set up then the interior is uploaded. As noted, although other types can be used, Lulu recommends for best results that a print-ready PDF is used with embedded fonts. Once this is uploaded, any problems which the system detects are corrected, and then the system prepares a print ready file for you to review. This can be downloaded and viewed in PDF format. At all stages you can return to previous sections and make changes.

The next section is the cover creator. This is slightly more limited than on CreateSpace however there are a number of designs you can work with or else you can upload your own cover design, using a similar template to that used in CreateSpace. Once you have completed this step then again you have a chance to review a print-ready copy and make changes, if required.

After this it is a simple matter of setting the distribution options (private access, direct access for a specific website or full sale via a range of outlets, including Amazon). If you select the latter option then you can set the retail price, giving you your required profit margin.

LIGHTNING SOURCE (LSI)

a. **Why choose LSI as a platform to publish your book:**

Lightning Source is another early type of POD publisher. It is a platform that is fairly and squarely aimed at the professional author/publisher, indeed it is marketed as a good way for the professional publisher to achieve professional looking results without the need for major investment in a publishing project, and to maintain an active back catalogue without the need to order expensive print runs.

This professional approach means that the requirements for Lightning Source are slightly more technical than for either Lulu or CreateSpace. If you can manage to deal with these requirements then you will get a very good result.

One great advantage which LSI has over other publishing platforms is that it distributes titles through Ingram, Bertrams, and all major networks. LSI also puts all their prints on Amazon giving maximum coverage to every title.

b. Requirements for Self-Publishing at LSI

Lightning Source does not support Microsoft Word or Publisher, Adobe Pagemaker or any of the other popular packages. Files have to be converted to font-embedded PDF formats. The PDF files have to be built to the trim size or in either letter or A4 size and in either PDF/X-1a:2001 or PDF/x-3:2002 format, with 600 dpi for 1-bit B&W text and 300dpi for 8-bit greyscale. Again if you're concerned about your ability to do this, consider using a company like The Fast Fingers.com who can format your book for you, they can be found at **http://www.thefastfingers.com**.

c. Steps for Self Publishing Your Book at LSI

After registration the steps to follow are fairly simple. The PDF textfile is uploaded or else you can send files to the company to be professionally scanned. There are a number of options available for publication:

Hardback books

Hardcover books are available in case laminate, cloth or jacketed in sizes: 216x140mm, 229x152mm, 234x156mm, 254x178mm, 280x216mm

Paperback books

Trade paperback books, available with perfect binding, are offered in the following sizes: 203 x 127 mm, 198 x 129 mm, 203 x 133 mm, 216 x 140 mm, 210 x 148 mm, 229 x 152 mm, 234 x 156 mm, 244 x 170 mm, 246 x 189 mm, 235 x 191 mm, 254 x 178 mm, 254 x 203 mm, 280 x 210 mm, 280 x 216 mm, 297mmx210mm

Colour books

Colour books are available in saddle-stitch, hardcover and perfect bindings starting with a page count of only 4 pages and sizes of: 216x140mm, 229x152mm, 234x156mm, 254x178mm, 254x203mm, 216x216mm, and 280x216mm.

The company also offers an academic or trade journal reprinting service.

As with all of the POD services, there is a guided option that will take you through the creation of the cover including the definition of the interior type, binding, paper and laminate type, book type and layout. You can also build the cover yourself and upload it using the Lightning Source template appropriate to your book trim size.

Once this is completed Lightning Source will print books and deliver them to your address, or market them on your behalf through trade channels.

Lightning Source is a very professional choice if you are looking for bigger print runs or for self-selling but lack the consumer driven element that CreateSpace or Lulu offer.

Let us see how Tony is getting on

Tony Ramos

Tony decided to publish his book through all three major publishing platforms namely Lulu.com, LSI and CreateSpace in order to maximise the distribution opportunities available to him and to ensure maximum sale of his book. As he had concerns about his ability to format his book himself and meet the specifications and requirements of all three platforms he sought the assistance of The Fast Fingers.com who helped him to edit and format his manuscript; they also created a bespoke book cover for him.

Although LULU does not provide much customer support, Tony got a free ISBN number there, and was able to upload his finished manuscript with ease. He also obtained a free ISBN from CreateSpace and uploaded his manuscript. As he had purchased a batch of 10 ISBNs from Nielsenbook he used one for his print at LSI. He also uploaded his manuscript to LSI.

Tony then obtained a printed copy of the book from all three publishing platforms in order to proof the print version of the book. He checked for errors such as typos, hanging headers, graphics, font size inconsistencies etc.

Tony made some adjustments to the manuscript then re-uploaded it to all 3 platforms. He then approved the final book. The book only took a few days before it was then made available for sale on all three platforms.

Your Turn

Now that you've got a completed manuscript, it's time to explore editing and formatting services if required and publishing options. Research the companies mentioned in this chapter and others you may find over the internet and write down some notes about each one in the following space:

Chapter 5

Digital Self-Published Books (e-books)

The previous chapter focused on self-publishing a printed book. This one will address some of the key differences in publishing a digital book.

Most publishing experts agree that digital publishing is the wave of the future. In fact, it's a wave that many are currently riding. With the advent of the Kindle, the Nook, the iPad, tablets, and other e-readers, people can buy and download hundreds of books and store them on a small reading device. Another advantage to digital publishing is that the content can be embedded with all kinds of extras like definitions, pop-up videos, and other links. Digital books are truly a multimedia experience. Even libraries and universities are offering books and textbooks as e-books these days.

So how can you capitalize on this trend? Is it just a matter of converting your existing manuscript to an e-book? Well, yes, and no.

Many of the publishers we mentioned in the last chapter will convert your book to an e-book for you. But, if you are looking to do it yourself, you will need to format your manuscript differently. You will want to make sure that your e-book looks the way you want it to.

There is also a very important thing to understand about the leading e-publishing services; they are not publishers. They are just distributors or retailers. That means they take no responsibility for the quality of your work, but neither do they take any rights to your work.

Here are some tips for formatting your manuscript for digital publication:

Don't use tabs or the space bar to format paragraphs or lines— It may look fine in Word, but it will appear off in digital print. Instead, use the "format/paragraph menu" to indent.

Use standard fonts—Times New Roman or Courier are good choices. Not all fonts are supported by digital readers. Also, use standard font sizes. 12 point is the standard. If the fonts are too big or too small they will appear irregular.

Use of images—When using images, keep them at about 300 pixels if you wish to show them in-line with your text. Also, resize your images using image editing software. Don't just make the text smaller within Word. Images should be in .jpg, .png, or .tif with 72 dpi and RGB colour mode. Don't wrap text around images.

Callout boxes or sidebars-Don't use callout boxes or sidebars. They won't display properly. Convert them into regular text.

Special symbols-Avoid the use of special symbols. Use your standard font for creating symbols.

Page numbers—remove any text that says, "See page ____" because the page numbers won't be the same on the e-reader as they are in the book.

File Formats

There are three main file formats used for digital books. They are:

.epub: This is the most common format. It's used by most retailers except for Amazon's Kindle. The benefit to it is that it allows for digital rights management, meaning that there are protections against someone sending your e-book to a friend for free.

.mobi: This is an e-book format that allow the user to add their own notes, text, bookmarks, et cetera.

.azw: This is the format used by Amazon.com for the Kindle. It does have digital rights management protections.

Recently Apple introduced the iBooks format (January 2013). You can create an e-book in the .ibooks format by using Apple's free iBooks Author software. These are especially formatted for tablets however there are two major drawbacks. Firstly at present they are only sold through iTunes and secondly they only work on Apple products.

Ironically, although PDFs are the preferred choice of POD publishers, they do not work well for digital publishing. Fortunately most digital publishers do the conversion for you from Word and .odt (Open and Libre Office) formats.

Which Format Should I Choose?

This is both a very difficult and quite easy question. It really depends upon how much time and effort you are willing to put into converting your texts to e-book formats and how many channels you wish to sell into.

Firstly, if you are seeking a single channel then the largest single market is Kindle. It was this format that really drove the revolution in e-books and there is no doubt that Amazon provides the biggest potential market exposure for self-published authors. The downside to the .azw file format is that it does not work with other e-readers such as Kobo, Nook or Sony; however there are free cross-platform applications for Android, PC and iPad devices.

If you have time, however, this need not be a problem; as you hold the rights to the book, there is nothing at all to stop you publishing across several if not all of the platforms. **Note however, if you use the Kindle platform and enrol for their optional KDP Select option to allow you to collect 70% of the royalties you receive on sales, you are required to publish exclusively on Kindle for periods of 90 days at a time.**

Digital Rights Management (DRM)

As we mentioned in the last section, Digital Rights Management is technology that allows publishers to prevent unauthorized use of digital media. These technologies provide copyright protection for authors who have created a digital product.

Although it's important to understand the concept of DRM, they are part of the publishing platform and not really something that the author deals with on his or her end. In other words, when you choose to publish with, say, Amazon, then Amazon.com handles the implementation of DRM with the end-user.

Some authors WANT their books to be freely shared as a form of marketing. If this is the case for you, then you can simply offer a free copy of your e-book as a download from your website.

Tony Ramos

Since Tony used all three platforms to publish his print book, he decided to choose LULU.COM only for his e-book as they have an ePub converter that automatically converted the file into the format he wanted. And, it was free. That worked very well for Tony!

Your Turn

Do you want to convert your paper book into an e-book? If so, would you rather use Amazon's formatting or another? Brainstorm your ideas in the space below.

Now that you have published your book via print-on-demand and electronically as an e-book it is now time to consider how you will market it.

PART 3

A Guide To Marketing A Book

Chapter 6

Book Marketing 101

It's the day you've been waiting for. You open the box and pull out a book that has your name on it! You are now officially a published author. Is it time to break out the champagne?

Right, But after you have a glass of celebratory bubbly it's time to set the glass down and get back to work. After all, writing and publishing the book are only half the battle. Now you have to get people to buy your book. It's not likely that you have a line of people around the block waiting to snap up your new release.

This chapter will cover some of the basic elements of book marketing. These are the kinds of things that every author needs to do—whether traditionally published or self-published.

Website

The first step in marketing your book is to create a website for it. While there is a lot more detail about creating an effective website than we can cover here, this section will contain the basics of what you need to consider when creating a website to sell your book.

If your book is designed to generate sales or is related to an existing business, then you can sell the book straight from your business website. If you are doing this, make sure to prominently display the book on the first page of your website and give visitors a way to purchase it. Your webmaster will be able to advise you on how to add a shopping cart to your site if you don't already have one. Many of the DIY website companies such as Go Daddy allow you to put these on your sites as well.

But, if your book is not related to your existing business, you'll need to create a website specifically for the book. Here are some considerations.

Domain name: If you can get it, choose the title of your book as your domain name. If that's taken, come up with some variation on it. Also, although other extensions are available, the first choice for a domain name is still .com as this is the most international option. If you can, get the other versions, too (either country specific e.g. .co.uk, .de etc. or .net, .info, et cetera). If not, do your best to get a .com.

In addition to getting the domain name, you'll need to have the website hosted somewhere. There are many different criteria you can use in selecting a web hosting company. You can look at price, you can go with one that has an easy to use website building template, you can find one that includes domain registration in the fees, or other items.

There is one really important caveat to note when choosing a web host. Make sure that you actually get a domain name, and not just an extension of the webhost's domain name. For example, Wix.com will offer you an easy to use website builder and free hosting. But, if you stay at the free level, your web address will be username.wix.com/domainname. If, for example, your book is called I Wrote A Best Seller, then you want the domain name iwroteabestseller.com, not username.wix.com/iwroteabestseller. Search engines won't be able to find your book unless you actually own the domain name.

In the case of Wix.com, and many other hosting sites, you can upgrade your service to include your own domain name.

Content: When choosing the content for your website, keep it exclusively to the book. This is not your personal page where you want to upload pictures of your kids and your vacation to Panama. This website is an advertising and sales vehicle for your book. Include testimonials, images of the book cover, and perhaps a downloadable sample chapter in exchange for someone's name and e-mail address. You want to capture their data for other kinds of marketing. Be sure and have a sign-up box for a mailing list.

Search Engine Optimization: make sure that your text is "SEO" friendly. SEO stands for Search Engine Optimization. What this means is that search engines, such as Google and Bing, crawl the Internet and catalogue websites based on the keywords that are in the site. So you want to make sure to very carefully use language that will allow the search engines to find your site and then bring it up as a result when someone enters that phrase into their search engine. So, for example, if your book is "I Wrote a Best Seller", you will want to include keywords that would bring that target audience to your book from the search engines. Think of what you would search for if you were looking for your own book. "Book writing," "best selling book" and "How to write a best seller" might be some good choices. Then, when you have that list, naturally use those phrases in your website. Don't be obvious about it. Just make it part of the language you choose to use on your website.

Video: You might consider adding a video element to your website. We'll talk more in the next chapter about using video to market your book. But research shows that websites with video get more traffic and more sales than those which don't.

Link exchange: Another item to help generate traffic for your website is the link exchange. You can approach other authors who have books you like and ask them to put a link to your website on their website in exchange for you doing the same with theirs. Not only does this give you visibility on their website, but the search engines will find your site on their site too. The more times your site appears on the Internet, the higher it will show up on the search engines. In other words, say you want to market your book I Wrote a Best Seller. You might approach your friend, the author of The Grammar Queen, and see if you can put iwroteabestseller.com on her website in exchange for you putting thegrammarqueen.com on your website. Then, when someone searches the term "grammar queen" your site will come up, too.

Overall, having an effective website is critical to the marketing of your book.

Book Reviews

Another powerful way to market your book is to get positive book reviews and post them on your website and other marketing materials. Many of the self-publishing houses have the option for you to purchase an independent review of your book.

In addition to being used as a marketing tool, this kind of input can actually improve the quality of the content of the book. iUniverse, for example, has a process called an Editorial Evaluation. It's a lengthy evaluation of your book that highlights the book's strengths and weaknesses. In the case of the Editorial Evaluation, the process is done prior to publication so that you can still make changes and edits based on the recommendations.

In addition to the reviews that might come with your publishing package, you can also solicit independent reviews of your book. There are several places you can go to get your book reviewed. Two of them are:

http://www.midwestbookreview.com
http://readerviews.com/submissions.html

In addition, you can send copies of your book to bloggers with a large following. Here is a link to a directory of bloggers.

http://bookbloggerdirectory.wordpress.com/fiction-blogs/general-fiction-poetry/gen-fic-poetry-a-h/

And, of course, you can encourage readers to write their own reviews on Amazon.com and Barnes and Noble.com, or wherever your book is sold online.

In March 2012, successful author, Christine Nolfi posted this useful advice to authors seeking reviews:

Recently I've been inundated with mail from other writers asking, "How did you get so many great reviews for your novels?"

The answer is straightforward. All it takes is patience and elbow grease. Trust me—you can do this. And if you can't afford the expense of a blog tour with a PR firm, this is a simple way to earn those much-deserved reviews.

Begin on Amazon. Find books similar to yours. A professional book reviewer will often list her full name on her review. She may also list the name of her book blog. Use either one for a Google search.

Once you've located the blog, read the Review Policy carefully. Follow the instructions on how to send a query. Put that information in an Excel or Word document with a contact and email address for the given reviewer.

Next, do a Google search of Book Blogs. Many directories are available. Yes, it takes time to scroll through the list, visit each site and read each

Review Policy. Also note that some blogs don't name the contact person in an About Me section. You'll have to read through several posts to find the name of the reviewer who runs the blog.

Once again, add these names to your Excel or Word list.

If you use Twitter (and I think you're crazy if you don't) you'll also bump into book reviewers. If a writer in your genre posts a review, pop over to the site and gather information. If a reviewer follows you, put her name in a Twitter List of potential reviewers. Use that list to add to your ever-growing Excel or Word list.

See the Christine Nolfi's *blog page for full details* **http://christinenolfibooks.blogspot.co.uk/2012/03/get-your-book-reviewed.html**

It almost goes without saying that if you want to receive positive reviews of your book you need to make sure that your book is good. Some unethical authors pay people to write positive reviews of their books and then use them as testimonials or on Amazon.com. But, in the end, if the book isn't any good, the truth will come out.

There is one particularly important source of reviews; Goodreads. Otis and Elizabeth Chandler founded Goodreads in December 2006 with an idea to give a place where book lovers could make friends with others who shared their love of reading. Rather than just relying on strangers, the members of Goodreads can see what their friends enjoy reading but, like any social networking site (which, fundamentally, is what it is) you can widen your circle of friends' way beyond the normal physical boundaries of your surroundings. Goodreads also facilitates discussions between members about books and is therefore a great place to start a 'buzz' about your writing.

Book Signings

One of the more traditional forms of book marketing is the book signing. A book signing is when the author goes to a location—usually a bookstore—and meets and greets the public, offering to personally sign copies of his or her book. You can also do book signings at trade shows, conferences, and other exhibits. For example, with your book I Wrote A Best Seller, you might do a book signing at the local book fair.

It's important to understand the purpose of a book signing. Contrary to what you might think, a book signing isn't about selling books. It's about selling yourself. You probably won't make a lot of money or sell a lot of books, but if you faithfully attend book signings, you'll start to build a loyal audience of readers.

Here is how to go about setting up a successful book signing:

Call to set up the signing: The first thing to do is to call to set up the signing. Choose a local bookstore or coffee house and call to see if they are interested. It's a good deal for the retail establishment because they get increased traffic. Alternatively, you can join a book signing with one or more additional authors so that you don't have to feel alone.

Then, once you've set a date, you either need to order the books yourself from your publisher or arrange for the venue to order them. Follow up by phone as needed, but don't do it so often that you're annoying.

Promote the book signing: Yes, the bookstore will be advertising it. But YOU are the one that your readers are interested in. So, promote it heavily. Tell your friends and family to tell their friends and family. Post it on Facebook, Twitter, and Linked In. Make up an insert to include in every piece of outgoing mail you have. Put it on the signature line of your e-mail. Change your voicemail greeting to include the book signing details. Send out a press release. The more you put into it, the more you will get out of it.

Don't overdress: Just wear nice, clean, casual clothes. You want to feel comfortable and like yourself.

Don't bring candy or cookies to put on your table: People will grab your food and not your book. You can bring other promotional items, though, if you have them. Bookmarks or other personalized things are a great touch.

Be friendly and smile: Invite people over to check out your book. You'd be surprised at what a friendly invitation will do. Remember, you're selling yourself, so focus on that and not your book.

Have a website: Having a website and conducting book signings are the basic ways that authors can promote their books. In the next chapter, we'll talk about some of the more advanced techniques.

Tony Ramos

Tony Ramos bought the domain name FlossingisFun.com to go along with his book Flossing is Fun. He put up a website using a simple web building tool. He used important key words like "floss" "dental health" "new flossing technique" and "the best way to floss" in his web copy. He got his friend Bob, the creator of fruit flavoured toothpaste to provide a link exchange. He did the same with several other friends.

Then, Tony conducted several books signings. He went to the annual dental conference, a health expo, and even did one at the local bookstore. Not only did Tony sell a few books, but he got a few new dental clients as well.

Your Turn

Do you have a website for your book? If not, check out the various domain names that could be available. Have you got friends or know people that you can set up a link exchange with? Have you considered book signing and where you can hold these? Write your ideas here:

Who might you get a link exchange with?

What are some relevant keywords for your web site?

Where might you go for book signings?

Where can you send your book for review?

Chapter 7

Advanced Marketing Techniques

In the last chapter you learned about the basic steps that every author should be taking to market his or her book. Those are the more passive marketing techniques. But, if you really want to boost your book sales, here are some of the more advanced marketing techniques. By "advanced," we don't mean hard. They are just a bit more time consuming on your part. But, as we mentioned earlier, the more you put into marketing your book the more you will get out of it. In this sense, time really is money.

Here are some additional ways you can market your book.

Internet Marketing

In the section on web design, you learned that it's important to have a place for you to capture visitor e-mail addresses. You can do this by offering them a sample chapter of the book, receipt of a newsletter or some other information product, or simply offering that they join your mailing list.

But, once you have their names and e-mail addresses, what do you do with them? Of course you must give them what was promised—the chapter, the information product, whatever . . . But, in addition to that, you can also use those names for an Internet marketing campaign.

To do this, you can write a monthly newsletter that highlights things that are relevant to your book. If your book is non-fiction, you can share trends and tips that help establish you as an expert. If your book is fiction, you can tell readers where you are going for book signings and share some testimonials for the book.

Also, you can create e-mail blasts with special discounts or other offers. Be careful with this, though. You don't want to overdo it or people will start to unsubscribe from your list.

Video

In a previous chapter, we suggested that you use video on your website to market your book. There are a few ways you can do this. First, you can create a video trailer of your book, just like the movie trailers you see in theatres. This can be an expensive option, though. For example, CreateSpace (an Amazon.com company) offers book trailer production from $1199-$2199. Author House offers their basic package for £1799 ($2699 in the US).

If you have some basic computer skills, though, you can create an effective book trailer yourself for no or low cost. For example, **Animoto.com** will allow you to create a 30 second video that you can post on your website for free. **Wevideo.com** also has a free option as well as some other low cost options. With a digital camera you can also create and edit an infomercial that you can upload to YouTube.

Perhaps the technology is a bit too much for you and you want to outsource it. You can hire a team to create an explainer video for you. Again, **Elance.com** and **Guru.com** are good sources for freelance video production talent.

Blog

In addition to creating a newsletter, you can also create a blog. This is an online journal of sorts. You can do a video blog or a written one. Again, it's a great way to establish yourself as an expert author. One tip though; do not constantly try to 'sell' or push your book. This tends to antagonise your readers.

Social Media

No marketing campaign is complete these days without social media. It's a good idea to create a Facebook page for your book, a Twitter account, and even a LinkdIn profile if your book is business related. As with your website, you want to keep the pages for the book separate from your personal social media pages. Instead, post interesting tidbits about the book, share your book signings and testimonials, and even share relevant quotes or passages. The key to effective social media marketing is consistency. Make sure that you are posting something every day or two.

And to refer back to the last chapter, remember Goodreads – the social network specifically designed for readers.

Public relations

The final advanced marketing technique we'll cover here is public relations, or PR. PR is a good way to get your name and book in the media for free.

Online press releases and traditional press releases offer a lot of exposure and buzz for your book. With them, you can reach potential buyers directly. You aren't likely to get a spot on ITV's This Morning or ABC's Good Morning America from your press release, but you can certainly get the search engines to find your book and website by using relevant keywords in your online press release.

Here is a template you can use when writing a press release for your book.

FOR IMMEDIATE RELEASE

Your Press Release Heading / Title Here

The first paragraph is a 2-4 sentence summary of what is newsworthy.

City, State – Date – The body of your press release starts here, on the same line as your dateline (the location and date). The first paragraph of your press release body should briefly answer the questions of who, what, when, where, and why.

The second paragraph should have a quote. This isn't a testimonial; it's a quote from you about why your book is relevant. "Readers need to know this kind of information," say you, the book author. "It's timely and important for everyone to know."

The third and final paragraph should give the additional details about your book, such as information about where the book is being distributed, its retail price, et cetera. Be sure and include the website address and contact information about yourself. Use your phone number so that it's easy for reporters to contact you.

End with ### to signify the end of the press release.

Once you've written the press release, you can send it to relevant newspaper reporters, online press release distribution agencies such as these:

http://media-newswire.com/

http://www.prweb.com/
http://www.newsbroadcastnetwork.com/
http://www.pressdispensary.co.uk/

Tony Ramos

Tony Ramos was excited to try the advanced marketing techniques. His dental practice had already been putting out a monthly newsletter, so it was easy for him to advertise his book that way. He also started a weekly blog called Flossing Fridays. On his home computer, Tony was able to use video editing software to create a professional looking book marketing video, which he placed on his website. He distributed press releases to the local newspapers and to the British and American Dental Association.

Your Turn

Which of the advanced marketing techniques appeal to you? Write them out here in the space below.

PART 4
Authors' Tips

Chapter 8

Common Mistakes Made In Writing, Self-Publishing And Marketing A Book

Well, there you have it. You've now learned everything you need to know about writing, self-publishing, and marketing your book. You're ready to go out into the world and start writing, right?

Not so fast. Before you put finger to keyboard, it's a good idea to identify the most common mistakes that authors make when writing, self-publishing and marketing their books. This chapter can help you avoid making these mistakes.

Mistake #1: Missing sections.

Make sure that you include all of the expected sections of the book, including the title page, copyright page, table of contents, et cetera. This can make the difference between a professional book and an amateur one.

Mistake #2: Thinking you can edit or proofread your own work.

No matter how great a writer you are, a professional proofreader can and will find mistakes that you have overlooked a hundred times.

Mistake #3: Missing the ISBN.

Be sure to put your ISBN inside of the book on the copyright page and also the ISBN and Bar Code on the back cover. You won't be able to sell the book in stores unless it's printed on the book.

Mistake #4: Telling too many "stories".

When writing your book, make sure that you stay focused on the reader and "what's in it for them." Even if you're writing a memoir, make sure to keep the content relevant to the reader and not just "and then we did this and then we went there."

Mistake #5: Point of View (POV) shifts.

This is especially relevant in fiction. Keep each paragraph and section to the perspective of one of the characters. When you shift, use a section or chapter break.

Mistake #6: An unprofessional appearance.

This is a very frequently occurring mistake. Make sure that your book looks professional. Don't use odd fonts, sizes, colours, strange characters, or smiley faces. Make sure your graphics are attractive and the right size for the page. Make sure that your fonts, line spacing, page breaks and formatting are consistent across the entire book.

Mistake #7: Documentation and reference problems.

Make sure that you give proper credit for the ideas and words of others. It's not okay to cut and paste sections from a website, Wikipedia, or another book and simply say where you got it. This includes photographs, graphics, and memes. You need written permission to use sections of copyrighted work. Also, if you cite a fact, a statistic, or a research study, you need to include the reference for where you found it. And, make sure you format the references properly.

Mistake #8: Thinking that marketing is a one-time deal.

You can't just put up a website, send out a press release, and do a book signing and be done with it. Marketing your book takes consistent, ongoing effort. The authors of the now-famous *Chicken Soup for the Soul* series were rejected by 123 publishers before it became an international best seller. They went from booth to booth at every bookseller convention in order to market their book.

Mistake #9: Not selling You.

Remember, YOU are the real thing being sold. It's your story, your expertise, or your personality that will sell books. People want a personal connection with the author, not just a book.

Mistake #10: Writing what you want to write and not what the market wants.

This is a hard one as one of the attractions of being an independent author is the lack of editorial interference, however if you want to sell books widely you need to produce what the market wants so you need to do your homework.

Mistake #11: Do not expect people to be as interested in your autobiography as you are!

This is a similar to the previous one but is more specific to non-fiction. Your life may well have been interesting but very few non-celebrity 'lifes' sell well.

Mistake #12: Giving up.

Writing, self-publishing, and marketing your own book can be a daunting task. But, don't give up. Persistence is the key to success. You can only fail if you quit. Until then, you have just learned what not to do.

Chapter 9

Key Points To Remember Before Writing, Self-Publishing And Marketing A Book

This is a checklist for you before you set out on your self-publishing adventure. Work through this list carefully and you will be in the best position to succeed in what you are setting out to do.

#1: Have you planned the layout, content, title and cover design of your proposed book?

Whether you are writing fiction or non-fiction, there is no doubt that having a good plan for the layout and content will improve the chances of you completing your project at all, and also bringing it in within your target time scale. If you can also decide on the title and what you would like on the cover then there will be nothing to delay the publication.

#2: Have you considered who would proof-read and edit your book?

As we have mentioned before, it is very hard to spot all mistakes in something you have written; it is worth finding a specialist, qualified proofreader to go through your book to ensure that it is as professional as possible. Do an online search for one or use a freelance site like Elance and get quotations. These quotations can be on an hourly rate or at an agreed fixed price.

Editorial work is different. An editor will look at the text, layout *and* content of your book and will give you objective advice on it. Conventional publishers will always ascribe an editor to a book project because they know that one is essential to ensure the book as a whole is as good as it can be.

Sometimes it is possible to find someone who can both edit and proofread though, strictly, they are two different professions.

#3 Do you know where to find your readers?

This will very much depend on what you are writing.

If it is a non-fiction book to promote you and your work you are probably going to aim this fair-and-square at your customers or peer group and you will be able to promote your book through your network (this is where applications like Linkdin, which is aimed at building up a network of professional/work contacts will come in really helpful).

If you are writing fiction then we suggest that you carefully review the sections on researching your subject area and market and also decide on how you are going to deliver it to them. Join Goodreads and read the discussions about books and genres similar to the ones you wish to produce. This will give you a very good idea of what your readership wants.

#4: Will your book meet your readers' expectations?

For both fiction and non-fiction, it is important to try and stand in your reader's shoes for a while. You need to see the book through *their* eyes, consider what *they* want out of it. With fiction, does your reader want pages and pages of pretty prose and descriptions? Possibly yes in a literary piece of work, almost certainly not in a fast-moving, Jack Reacher/ Jason Bourne type of adventure novel. In non-fiction, are you pitching the material at too high a level, risking confusing them, or too low and insulting their intelligence. Are you explaining things well? Are you just dazzling them with your brilliance and expertise yet not telling them anything that they will actually be able to gain value from?

Sometime it is hard to be objective about this. It is always worthwhile getting other people to read at least some of your material and get their honest opinion.

#5: Is your book going to be a Print on Demand/e-book or both?

As we have seen, the formatting and distribution characteristics of each tend to be rather different. In some books, particularly non-fiction books with lots of detailed illustrations, you may find that the e-book format will not work successfully.

#6: Have you priced your book realistically and reasonably to ensure maximum book sales?

If too costly, there will be fewer buyers despite many showing an interest, though, oddly, many cheap books get overlooked by readers because they feel that anything priced so low cannot be worthwhile!

#7: Have you prepared yourself for the time, effort and money required to get your book published?

You will have to spend quality time getting out a quality book to your readers; this is a considerable investment in your time, if nothing else. If you also have to make a living whilst writing, editing, producing and marketing your book you will have to develop strong time-management skills in order to prioritise effectively.

Furthermore, you will have to cover the cost of proofreading, editorial and formatting serves; these expenses are not cheap.

#8: Have you considered how to reach your target market?

Sadly, a common failure of many books is 'The Field of Dreams' issue; not so much 'If I build it, they will come' but 'if I write it, they will buy it'! The task (an achievement, once completed) of writing a book tends to dominate a writer's world so much that they overlook this key element. What is your market? Who are you writing the book for? How do you reach them?

Once you have asked these questions, and come up with what seem to be sensible answers, this then leads onto the next point.

#9: What are your promotion or marketing strategies?

As a self-published author, unless you are a marketing expert, this is the most difficult of areas. To be completely successful you may have to devote as much time to this as you did to writing the book in the first place.

#10: Have you considered possible setbacks, lack of recognition from expected quarters and critical reviews. How would you deal with the rejection of your book?

Most of the previous points are largely positive, however not everything in the garden is rosy. You must be prepared for the downsides of writing and self-publishing. These can range from critical reviews to, if you have gone too far, legal action. Admittedly, the latter is unlikely unless you have defamed some person or company, however the former IS likely. How you approach this depends upon you as an individual, but above all, you should try to be as objective as possible. Ask yourself, is the criticism valid? Are there changes I can make to address the problems that the critic has made? Or are the criticisms unfair? Have they failed to read your book properly or are there vested interests involved – a rival business or author.

A self-published author should ideally be sensitive and receptive to valid criticism whilst being thick-skinned and confident enough to stand by their work so you are not changing the material to suit everyone's opinion. Remember, it is virtually impossible to produce something that everyone will like. Still, this is often a hard path to follow; criticism of your writing is like your children being criticized by others. It can be hard to take!

#11: If you intend to order too many print on demand copies expecting huge sales, what will you do with the books if they are not sold?

You may have to make provision for storage – and books can take up a lot of space – but, if you have done your market research correctly, this should not happen. The whole point about Print-on-Demand is that it is just that; you should only have to order the amount of books you actually need.

#12: Have you considered the running costs i.e. book cover design, proof reading, editing, formatting, uploading to Publishing sites and Marketing costs; how will these be funded?

This is particularly important if the book is part of your business or professional promotion programme; like anything in business, it should be properly planned and budgeted.

#13: Have you considered giving your manuscript to professionals, family members to critique pre—submission for their honest, constructive feedback and reviews?

Using family members and friends can be helpful if they can be relied upon to give honest, constructive feedback and reviews; if you are going to get treated with kid-gloves because they do not want to hurt your feelings then the process is not going to genuinely help you.

If you are a fiction writer, this is where being in a mature, critical writing group can really help. They will not read the whole manuscript but you will certainly get pointers which will guide you towards improvement. If you can afford it, using the services of a critique service will be invaluable. Beware though, there are many charlatans offering expensive but largely worthless services. One good one for fiction is Cornerstones (**http://www.cornerstones.co.uk**). For non-fiction, hiring an editor will improve the professionalism of what you produce.

#14: Finally, remember that writing your own book and seeing it in print or out listed in e-book form is an intensely satisfying experience.

Publishing platforms are more accessible than ever before and the stigma that used to be associated with self-publishing is rapidly diminishing. If you have something to say, you have a right to have your voice heard. Self-publishing gives you the opportunity for your voice to be heard. Don't be discouraged; be brave, publish those books and have the satisfaction of seeing your name in print!

Chapter 10

Useful Resources

Here are the resources mentioned throughout in this book.

General Resources

Freelancers (editors, proof readers, video and web pages etc)

Elance—**www.elance.com**

Guru – **http://www.guru.com/**

Writer's Digest—**www.writersdigest.com**

Onetwofiver.com—**http://onetwofiver.com/about/**

Self-publishing companies

Author House—**www.authorhouse.co.uk** and **www.authorhouse.com**

Troubador—**www.troubador.co.uk**

Author Solutions—**www.authorsolutions.com**

Niche publishers

Westbow—**www.westbowpress.com** (Christian publishers)

Dellarte Press—**http://www.pressdispensary.co.uk/** (Romance and women's interest)

Self-publishing platforms

LULU – **www.lulu.com**

Create Space—**www.createspace.com**

Lightning Source – **www.lightningsource.com**

General Useful Resources

Book formatting—**www.thefastfingers.com**

ISBN issue—**www.isbn.org/standards/home/index.asp**

Book reviews

http://www.midwestbookreview.com

http://readerviews.com/submissions.html

http://bookbloggerdirectory.wordpress.com/fiction-blogs/general-fiction-poetry/gen-fic-poetry-a-h/

Videos

www.animoto.com

www.wevideo.com

Press Releases

http://media-newswire.com/

http://www.prweb.com/

http://www.newsbroadcastnetwork.com/

http://www.pressdispensary.co.uk/

Critiques

http://www.cornerstones.co.uk/

CONCLUSION

Thanks so much for reading this book. We hope you enjoyed it and have learned all you need to know in order to effectively write a good book, self-publish, and market it yourself.

We would like to wish you the best of luck and every success with your publishing venture.

If you have found this book useful, kindly provide your reviews on the website you purchased a copy of this book from or the various publishing platforms such as Amazon, CreateSpace and Lulu.

Other Books by Authors

The Beginners' Guide to Wealth Creation

A Simple Guide to UK Immigration

Become All That God Has Created You To Be

Hearing God's Voice

You Are Blessed

Purpose2Destiny TK Limited

P O BOX 3162

Romford

RM3 9WR

United Kingdom

www.ingramcontent.com/pod-product-compliance
Lightning Source LLC
Chambersburg PA
CBHW070648050426
42451CB00008B/314